COOL CAREERS WITHOUT COLLEGE
FOR PEOPLE WHO LOVE TO
COOK & EAT

NEW

COOL CAREERS WITHOUT COLLEGE
FOR PEOPLE WHO LOVE TO
COOK & EAT

SARAH MACHAJEWSKI

ROSEN
PUBLISHING®

New York

Published in 2014 by The Rosen Publishing Group, Inc.
29 East 21st Street, New York, NY 10010

First Edition

Library of Congress Cataloging-in-Publication Data

Machajewski, Sarah.
Cool careers without college for people who love to cook & eat/Sarah Machajewski.—First edition.
    pages cm.—(New cool careers without college)
Audience: Grades 7–12.
Includes bibliographical references and index.
ISBN 978-1-4777-1820-9 (library binding)
1. Food service—Vocational guidance—Juvenile literature. 2. Restaurants—Vocational guidance—Juvenile literature. 3. Cooks—Juvenile literature. I. Title.
TX911.3.V62M33 2014
647.95023—dc23

2013011087

Manufactured in the United States of America

CPSIA Compliance Information: Batch #W14YA: For further information, contact Rosen Publishing, New York, New York, at 1-800-237-9932.
A portion of the material in this book has been derived from *Cool Careers Without College for People Who Love Food* by Kerry Hinton.

CONTENTS

INTRODUCTION

Pizza. Pasta. Mac and cheese. Cake. Cookies. Did the mention of any of these foods make your mouth water? It's not surprising if it did. All of these foods are delicious when you eat them, but sometimes even the mere mention of food can make you feel happy and excited—especially if you're hungry! Food is a special thing in this world, in that the love of it unites all people: no matter how different people's lives are, everybody likes to eat.

Few people view eating as a chore. In fact, most of us look forward to our next meal. Imagine how long the day would seem without taking a break for three square meals (and snacks). We all know that we have to eat in order to live, but food does more than give our bodies energy: it brings people together, helps us celebrate holidays, gives us something to talk about, and can be a mode of creative expression. In this fast-paced world, the kitchen, dining room, or restaurant table may be one of the few places for everyone to gather at the same time. Now imagine if you could be involved in providing this shared experience to others. Sounds cool, right?

If you like cooking meals for your family and friends, experimenting with recipes and cooking techniques, and

Getting a job in the food industry may seem easy, but keeping it requires hard work and commitment. Do you have what it takes?

helping people relax in a pleasant environment with good food, you may want to consider a career that involves the buying, preparing, and selling—and hopefully eating—of food. Luckily, there are many jobs based on and around it.

The food industry is huge, and the number of professions within it may surprise you. In the following sections, we've covered some practical jobs, some jobs that can turn into lifelong careers, and even some fun jobs you may have never heard of. Almost all the jobs in this book can be attained with just a high school diploma or minimal training. However, working in the food industry is not easy. It requires a strong work ethic, dedication, and of course, an appetite!

CHAPTER 1

RESTAURANT STAFF: WAITING TABLES AND MORE

One of the easiest ways to break into the food industry is with an entry-level job in a restaurant. For teens and young adults looking for their first job, the obvious choice may be a hosting or serving gig at a local restaurant. Although the job of a food server may seem simple, it's by no means easy.

Food servers—waiters and waitresses—require thorough knowledge of almost every aspect of a restaurant's operation in order to be efficient and effective at their jobs. Good people skills are a requirement, too. The physical and emotional demands placed on food servers can be taxing, but it's a great source of income for young people looking for job experience.

While hosts and hostesses aren't heavily involved with the food itself, it's often a stepping-stone to becoming a waiter or waitress. And that's where the real fun begins!

SERVICE WITH A SMILE

Food servers are the direct link between customers and a restaurant's kitchen. From the time customers are seated, their server influences a good portion of their experience. One of the most important parts of gaining and keeping a serving job is the ability to provide "service with a smile." Customer service is how you treat and interact with customers. Excellent customer service is going the extra mile to accommodate their requests and needs. Most servers will tell you that good customer service is all about being polite, friendly, and most of all, patient. Because customers interact with servers more than anyone else in a restaurant, these qualities—or the lack thereof—can greatly impact the restaurant's reputation.

This waiter's great customer service, shown by his smile and welcoming attitude, makes his customer feel at ease.

Food servers are expected to take orders, serve food, and set and clear tables. Above all, servers must communicate messages between customers and the kitchen. Successful servers familiarize themselves with the menu and how menu items are prepared. It helps in answering customer questions and helping them choose something they'll enjoy. For example, a server can warn customers with allergies against ordering certain dishes or tell the kitchen to alter menu items for customers with dietary restrictions. Depending on the restaurant, they may be required to know more. Servers in ethnic restaurants may have to interpret the menu for diners who are unfamiliar with the cuisine. In upscale restaurants, a food server may be asked to recommend the best wines to complement a meal or even perform some food preparation at customers' tables. Did someone say "guacamole"?

Serving jobs are available in several different environments. Where you choose to work depends on where you'd be most comfortable. Coffee shop employees must be fast and efficient, since customers are in a hurry. Being able to work under pressure is a benefit here. On the other end of the spectrum, high-end restaurants offer a more leisurely dining experience. Customers here expect impeccable and knowledgeable service from servers who won't rush them. There are also many restaurants between these two extremes.

Many people choose to wait tables because the flexible schedule gives them time to pursue other interests. Servers are often students who need part-time work, parents who have other responsibilities, or people in creative fields such as acting who need a steady income. A serving job is flexible enough that you can make money and dedicate your time elsewhere. The drawback is that people who wait tables rarely have a consistent weekly schedule. Shifts may change or be called off without warning. In addition, food servers know that they may be asked to work very early or very late, even if they aren't scheduled to do so ahead of time.

Another thing to consider before taking a serving job is that the work is very physical. Servers are always on their

You can spot a server by the heavy trays of food that she must carry around the restaurant. Good balance is a must!

feet and spend a lot of time walking back and forth between tables and the kitchen, often with heavy trays of food and drinks. If you have back problems or get tired easily, this career is not the best choice.

Based on what you've read so far, you probably know if a serving job fits your personality. A word of warning, though: if you have trouble dealing with people, this is not the job for you. No matter how many times you have to clean up a spill or how rude a particular customer may be, your job depends on the "three C's"—being cool, calm, and collected.

WHAT DOES IT TAKE TO BECOME A FOOD SERVER?

Serving jobs rarely require formal education or training. This makes them a great option for teens who are still in high school or for anybody who wants to see if the food industry is the right fit for them. A big part of getting hired for a restaurant's waitstaff is the ability to learn as you go. Many restaurants have a brief orientation to help servers become comfortable with the specifics of their operations, but they expect new employees to learn the ropes quickly.

A person's first serving job is unlikely to be at a high-end restaurant. These establishments require a good deal of waiting experience. Waiters and waitresses at the most fancy

FINE DINING 101

Many servers aspire to hold a job in an upscale restaurant. It can be a lucrative gig: the money is better, the environment is more luxurious, and there's a chance you'll work with some of the highest quality food around. But excelling as a fine-dining server is no easy task. Some of the fine-dining etiquette that servers must follow includes:

- **Welcoming guests.** Servers must introduce themselves to the table with their name, letting the customers know they will be taking care of them for the evening. They provide menus and a thorough explanation of the night's specials.

- **Establishing rapport.** It's a good idea for servers to make conversation with their tables. This makes the diners feel comfortable and welcomed, which can lead to more generous tips. A conversation starter can be asking if the table is out for a special occasion or what they're looking forward to having. Servers must be careful to not overstep their boundaries, though. Being too chatty can be annoying to some diners.

- **Serving the meal.** Fine-dining etiquette states that service starts on the right and moves in a clockwise direction around the table. The exception is if the food is being served family style, in which case service goes to the left. A general rule of thumb is that women are served before men. Further, at special events like weddings, the guests of honor are served first.

- **Keeping a neat table.** Servers are expected to clear the table between courses and all at once. Experienced servers know not to take away plates or glasses from one diner while the other is still eating so as to avoid rushing the meal. Servers will also clear the table of crumbs or even replace a tablecloth if it appears to be dirty.

- **Presenting the bill.** Handling the check can sometimes be an awkward situation for diners and servers alike. Servers always present the check after the meal, dessert, and after-dinner drinks are finished—never before. In fine-dining situations, the presentation of the bill must be discreet and not attention grabbing.

restaurants must perform the basics perfectly before they can perform more complicated tasks.

Your best bet is to start off with a part-time job as a waiter or waitress while you're in school. Many local and chain restaurants can accommodate school schedules and are prepared to train you in the basics. Holding a part-time serving job is a valuable experience for those interested in a culinary career. It gives you a great advantage later on if you decide to pursue other roles in the food industry.

PAY AND JOB PROSPECTS FOR FOOD SERVERS

Have you ever heard of something called the minimum wage? If you want to be a server, forget it! In most restaurants, waiters and waitresses have a base salary that is far below the federal minimum wage. It's often just a couple of dollars. The real money-making opportunity is found in the tips. Most customers know that servers depend on tips. In

Fine-dining servers work hard for their tips, but the payoff can be worth it.

the United States, it's customary for servers to receive between 15 and 20 percent of the final bill as their payment.

Restaurants that have a wealthier clientele and more expensive menus may pay a higher hourly wage. What's more, fine-dining servers can expect to make good tips because the food and drinks are usually more expensive in these kinds of establishments. Be aware, though, that as a server you're often expected to split your tips with the rest of the house. At the end of the night, servers give some of their tips to the hosts, bartenders, and busboys who aided them in serving their tables.

While the majority of waitstaff jobs don't provide medical or retirement benefits, they may offer different perks, such as free or discounted meals. Some restaurants also provide uniforms for their employees.

According to the most recent edition of the *Occupational Outlook Handbook*, the outlook is good for waiters and waitresses. Waiting jobs are usually plentiful. Due to the high turnover rate in the field, many restaurants are always hiring new employees. There are usually a number of restaurants in one town, so talented servers can often choose the kind of restaurant they'd like to work in. What's more, as more and more people go out to eat, restaurants are growing and hiring bigger staffs to accommodate the increase in business.

FOR MORE INFORMATION

ORGANIZATIONS

Canadian Restaurant and Foodservices Association (CRFA)
316 Bloor Street W
Toronto, ON M5S 1W5
Canada
(800) 387-5649
Web site: http://www.crfa.ca
The CRFA represents all sectors of the Canadian food service industry, including restaurants, bars, cafeterias, coffee shops, caterers, and more.

National Restaurant Association (NRA)
2055 L Street NW, Suite 700
Washington, DC 20036
(202) 331-5900
Web site: http://www.restaurant.org
The National Restaurant Association represents almost four hundred thousand restaurants, providing valuable resources and information to all levels of food industry employees.

National Restaurant Association Educational Foundation
175 West Jackson Boulevard, Suite 1500

Chicago, IL 60604-2814
(800) 765-2122
Web site: http://www.nraef.org
This organization supports the National Restaurant
   Association in offering professional development,
   education, licensing, and certification in restaurant
   occupations.

Occupational Safety and Health Administration (OSHA)
U.S. Department of Labor
200 Constitution Avenue NW
Washington, DC 20210
(800) 321-OSHA [6742]
Web site: http://www.OSHA.gov
The Occupational Safety and Health Administration
   of the U.S. Department of Labor generated a special
   Web site, http://www.osha.gov/SLTC/youth/restaurant
   /index.html, to educate young restaurant workers
   about staying safe in the workplace.

BOOKS

Arduser, Lora, and Douglas Robert Brown. *The Waiter
   & Waitress and Waitstaff Training Handbook: A Complete Guide to the Proper Steps in Service for Food &*

Beverage Employees. Ocala, FL: Atlantic Publishing Group, 2005.
This training handbook explores all aspects of customer service for food servers, including step-by-step instructions for a variety of skills.

Caletti, Deb. *The Fortunes of Indigo Skye*. New York, NY: Simon & Schuster Books for Young Readers, 2008.
In this fiction title, eighteen-year-old Indigo is looking forward to becoming a full-time waitress after high school graduation, but her life is turned upside down by the act of a customer.

Dublanica, Steve. *Waiter Rant: Thanks for the Tip—Confessions of a Cynical Waiter*. New York, NY: Ecco, 2008.
The author provides a humorous account of what it's really like to be a waiter. Outrageous and funny stories teach readers the best way to provide good service, even when people don't deserve it!

Sanders, Edward E. *The Professional Server: A Training Manual*. 2nd ed. Boston, MA: Pearson, 2012.
This book covers everything a good server needs to know in order to succeed in this profession.

BLOGS

Restaurant Laughs

http://www.restaurantlaughs.com

This blog offers a collection of humorous restaurant stories, showing both the good and bad sides of waiting tables.

Stuck Serving

http://www.stuckserving.com

This blog collects and publishes readers' stories about their experiences as servers. Sure to make you laugh, this blog will surprise you with its stories about waiting tables.

WEB SITES

Due to the changing nature of Internet links, Rosen Publishing has developed an online list of Web sites related to the subject of this book. This site is updated regularly. Please use this link to access the list:

http://www.rosenlinks.com/CCWC/Cook

CHAPTER 2

LIFE AS A RESTAURANT MANAGER

Restaurants are very busy places. Between feeding customers, employing a full staff, keeping up with inventory, and making the business profitable, there is a lot to think about when it comes to a restaurant's operations. The person who oversees all of these things is typically the restaurant manager.

Restaurant managers are constantly pulled in different directions. Good restaurant managers must be in control and aware of almost everything that occurs in the workplace. They must be able to delegate tasks and ensure a positive experience for the people in the restaurant—everyone from customers to employees.

It takes a special kind of person to be a successful restaurant manager. You have to enjoy working with people and have a knack for customer service. You may even need a basic understanding of the business side of the restaurant. If you don't mind long hours and a lot of responsibility—and you can handle stress—this may be the career for you.

CLIMBING THE RESTAURANT LADDER

Managing a restaurant requires organization, a solid understanding of basic business principles, and a thorough understanding of how the food service industry operates.

At the heart of a restaurant manager's responsibilities is ensuring smooth coordination between the floor staff and the kitchen staff.

Most managers start in entry-level service positions and work their way up over time. The benefit of this experience is that they come to the job with an understanding of what the working conditions are for the people they manage. At the same time, the role of running a restaurant separates the manager from the rest of the employees. Staff members have to view the manager as a superior rather than a coworker. And managing others includes responsibilities that can be unpleasant. For example, a restaurant manager may have to fire people who can't obey basic rules like showing up on time, or worse, employees who are stealing from the business.

Restaurant managers also need to know a lot about food. Although managers don't directly prepare the food, they usually choose suppliers, approve of and order ingredients, and do these things while adhering to a previously determined food budget. Further, the manager may work with chefs and

On a busy night, a Denver restaurant manager helps carry out plates from the kitchen.

cooks to come up with creative ideas, such as menu items and promotions. All of these things help the restaurant turn a profit.

Be prepared to work quite a few hours if you choose to be a restaurant manager. While it's a fun and interesting job, you may be called upon to handle unplanned crises. If the ice machine breaks or if a pipe in the men's restroom bursts, you can't go home, even if your shift is almost over. Managing a restaurant can also be stressful, as customer complaints and employee issues are often passed along to the person in charge. As with a food server, patience is key in this role.

As a restaurant manager, you must go into the job knowing that it's a lot of work. You are responsible for everything that goes on in the restaurant, so if work is not accomplished, you are ultimately to blame. It takes exceptional personal skills to know how to delegate tasks

Most managers use the time before a restaurant opens or after it closes to do important tasks, such as ordering supplies and planning schedules.

and see them through to completion. To help with this, good managers try to foster a team environment. If employees feel that their manager supports and encourages them, they'll be more willing to do a good job.

WHAT DOES IT TAKE TO BECOME A RESTAURANT MANAGER?

Many managers start in entry-level positions, beginning their careers as cooks, hosts, bartenders, or food servers.

This allows them to become familiar with the inner workings of a restaurant, which helps them as they work their way up to a management position. Previous restaurant experience is important because it gives managers a better understanding of their employees and the challenges of their jobs. The average restaurant manager spends three or four years in the trenches, gaining all the knowledge needed to run a restaurant.

A college degree is not necessary for obtaining a restaurant manager's job. Restaurant owners are more likely to hire someone without a degree who has been in the business for a long time versus someone with a degree but no experience or prior professional relationship with the owner.

PAY AND JOB PROSPECTS FOR RESTAURANT MANAGERS

The average restaurant manager makes a salary rather than an hourly wage. Salaries are determined by the city in which one works, since the cost of living is different for every city. A manager's salary can also depend on how long he or she has been with the business, the exact nature of the responsibilities, and how much time the manager spends at the restaurant. As a manager's responsibilities grow, it's possible to negotiate a higher salary to match the job duties.

DAY MANAGERS VS. NIGHT MANAGERS

Restaurants are open at all different times of the day. Some establishments are open only for dinner, some places only do breakfast, and others are open for twenty-four hours. If a restaurant is open for more than one meal, it will usually staff more than one manager to cover all of its hours of operation. One manager will cover the opening of the restaurant, and the other will cover the closing. The opening shift is very different from the closing shift, and managers' duties and responsibilities vary based on which one they cover.

As an opening manager, be prepared to get up very early. This shift is dedicated to one thing and one thing only: preparing the restaurant to open. Managers and other restaurant staff use the few short hours before the doors open to get the food and the space ready for customers. This can involve chopping produce or preparing large quantities of menu items that aren't made to order. Opening managers (sometimes referred to as "morning" or "day" managers) may also ready the dining area of the restaurant by setting tables and stocking items such as napkins and condiments. Ultimately, the managers are there to see that everything goes off without a hitch and that the restaurant is fully prepared to take on the day's customers.

Closing managers have quite the daunting job: they oversee all aspects of shutting the restaurant down. Can you imagine how much there is to do? Closing managers make sure that the restaurant is cleaned thoroughly, the floors are mopped or vacuumed, and the garbage is taken out. They also make sure

that food is properly stored and that nothing is left out to spoil or become contaminated. Some restaurants use the closing shift to prepare food for the next day. This can involve anything from slicing lemons to baking bread. Closing managers have one more very important job: counting the day's earnings. This is a lot of responsibility, and it is usually reserved for the most trusted of managers.

Night managers must make sure the restaurant is clean before shutting down for the day. If an employee doesn't mop, the manager will.

Management opportunities are plentiful for people in the food industry who decide to stick it out, if only because of the high turnover rate. People who work at a restaurant (or several restaurants) in varying roles are likely to become managers one day. If you think this career sounds interesting, give it a try, but remember to be patient. The longer you work for a restaurant, the better equipped you'll be to take on a managerial role, should it become available.

FOR MORE INFORMATION

ORGANIZATIONS

National Restaurant Association (NRA)
2055 L Street NW, Suite 700
Washington, DC 20036
(202) 331-5900
Web site: http://www.restaurant.org
The National Restaurant Association represents almost four hundred thousand restaurants, providing valuable resources and information to food industry employees.

Restaurant Facility Management Association (RFMA)
5600 Tennyson Parkway, Suite 280
Plano, TX 75024
(972) 805-0905
Web site: http://www.rfmaonline.com
The RFMA works to promote the advancement of the restaurant facility management professional. It provides excellent resources for people in this role.

Society for Foodservice Management (SFM)
455 South 4th Street, Suite 650
Louisville, KY 40202
(502) 574-9931

Web site: http://www.sfm-online.org
This national association serves the needs and interests
of executives in the onsite food service industry. It
also includes faculty and students at hotel, restaurant,
and institutional management programs.

BOOKS

Adams, Angela C. *The Restaurant Manager's Success
Chronicles: Insider Secrets and Techniques Food Service
Managers Use Every Day to Make Millions*. Ocala, FL:
Atlantic Publishing Group, 2008.
This book reveals insider secrets related to restaurant
management.

The Culinary Institute of America. *Remarkable Service:
A Guide to Winning and Keeping Customers for Servers,
Managers, and Restaurant Owners*. 2nd ed. Hoboken,
NJ: Wiley, 2009.
This book is a comprehensive guide to all aspects of a
restaurant's operations.

Garvey, Michael, H. Dismore, and Andrew Dismore. *Running a Restaurant for Dummies*. 2nd ed. Hoboken, NJ:
Wiley, 2011.

This volume teaches readers how to run a restaurant in a relatable and fun way.

Meyer, Danny. *Setting the Table: The Transforming Power of Hospitality in Business*. Paperback ed. New York, NY: Harper, 2008.
Danny Meyer's best-selling book offers expert advice for anyone planning to work in the food service industry.

Reynolds, Dennis E., and Kathy McClusky. *Foodservice Management Fundamentals*. Hoboken, NJ: Wiley, 2013.
This book shows readers how to manage a successful food service operation in a variety of venues.

PERIODICALS

Food Management
Penton Media
1300 East 9th Street
Cleveland, OH, 44114
(216) 696-7000
Web site: http://food-management.com
Food Management offers ideas, news, and resources for food service management professionals and chefs.

FSR

Web site: http://www.fsrmagazine.com

FSR magazine is a print publication that provides ideas and insights for chefs, owners, executives, and decision-makers in the full-service restaurant industry. A subscription is free for those who work in the full-service restaurant industry.

Nation's Restaurant News

1166 Avenue of the Americas, 10th Floor

New York, NY 10036

Web site: http://www.nrn.com

(212) 204-4200

This magazine's print and online content covers industry news, franchise information, and upcoming trade show schedules.

SLAMMED Magazine

190 Lincoln Street

Hingham, MA 02043

(781) 749-9005

Web site: http://www.slammedmagazine.com

This magazine offers a youthful and fun take on all aspects of the restaurant industry.

BLOGS

The Restaurant Manager's Rant
http://therestaurantmanagersrants.blogspot.com
This blog gives a firsthand account of what it's like to be
   a restaurant manager.

The Manager's Office
http://www.themanagersoffice.com
A free resource for restaurant managers, this blog offers
   tips, tricks, and general information on the trade.

WEB SITES

Due to the changing nature of Internet links, Rosen Publishing has developed an online list of Web sites related to the subject of this book. This site is updated regularly. Please use this link to access the list:

http://www.rosenlinks.com/CCWC/Cook

CHAPTER 3

FILLING ORDERS AS A COOK

Do you like to cook? Do you find your friends and family always asking you to make them dinner? If so, a career as a cook may be something to look into. Before you start planning menus and donning a tall chef's hat, though, you must know that there is a huge difference between a chef and a cook. We'll talk about what chefs do a little later. For now, we'll go behind the scenes in an average kitchen, where cooks whip up a huge number and variety of dishes in one short shift.

Cooks are found anywhere food is, in places such as diners, chain restaurants, burger joints, and fast-food restaurants. Many large institutions have kitchens that employ cooks, such as hospitals, office buildings, camps, and even your own school's cafeteria. If you can see yourself in any of these places, one way to get there is by becoming a cook.

ORDER UP!

Unlike chefs who plan menus and experiment with recipes, cooks work from a previously created menu and rarely offer

A grill cook prepares meat, fish, and chicken for the employee cafeteria at Google headquarters in California.

input into what goes into the recipes. It's a known rule that cooks can't deviate from the menu or recipes provided by the restaurant. The reasons for this are varied, but it mostly comes down to consistency. This is especially true in chain restaurants and fast-food joints, where dishes have to exactly match what the corporate entity determines them to be. This

WHAT'S IN A NAME?

There are many kinds of cooks, and they all handle something different in the kitchen. Cooks gets their names from the stations they man. It can get pretty crowded in there, so knowing who the various cooks are and what they do will make your first day on the job a little less intimidating. Typical cooks include:

- **Line cook.** This is the general term for anybody who prepares meals in a kitchen who isn't a chef. Line cooks are also known as chefs de partie.
- **Sauté cook.** *Sauté* is a French word that means "to cook quickly in a pan with butter or another fat," and sauté cooks do just that. You'll often see them flipping vegetables high into the air to get a good crisp on them.
- **Fry cook.** Fry cooks are often depicted in movies and TV as the fast-food workers who flip burgers and drop french fries in the fryer. They generally take care of any greasy fried food that comes out of the kitchen.
- **Grill cook.** These cooks work with meat and usually come to the job with some training in the art of grilling. They give steak, chicken, fish, and other proteins the delicious char-grilled flavor that people love.
- **Cold foods cook.** Cold foods cooks take care of anything fresh and crisp. This includes prepping salads, cold sandwiches, fruit courses, and other dishes that don't require an oven or a stove.

helps fulfill customer expectations and maintain the business's brand identity.

A cook's main responsibility is to prepare food on an as-needed basis, filling orders as they come in from the waitstaff. Nowadays, most food is made to order, so cooks have to be efficient and practiced in preparing a meal in which all components of the dish are hot, tasty, and ready to go at the same time. This gets even more complicated when there are multiple orders per table. Not all menu items are made to order, though. Some foods such as stews, soups, and sauces can be prepared in advance, making a cook's life easier. They are often made in bulk at the start of a day or shift and are dispensed as they are requested.

If you think about the qualities that make a successful cook, one of the first that should pop into your mind is cleanliness. Cooks must be extremely conscious of maintaining a clean workspace. Because they directly handle the food that people will eat and enjoy, cooks must be aware of food storage rules and how to prevent cross-contamination of food. For example, some dishes cannot be served with the utensils used to prepare the raw ingredients. An absent-minded cook may purposefully prepare a dish that has no allergens in it but use equipment that came into contact with nuts, dairy, or other ingredients off-limits to customers.

Doing this could make certain people very sick. This is serious business, and it takes a dedicated cook to remember to apply all guidelines and regulations regarding health and sanitation.

There are several different kinds of cooks. Short-order cooks fill orders as they come in. Their counterpart is the institutional cook. Institutional cooks have a very similar job, but they prepare huge volumes of food. Think about all of the people in hospitals, schools, and office buildings. All of these places have dozens, maybe even hundreds, of employees and visitors who eat at roughly the same time once or twice a day. That's a lot of meals! Most institutional cooks have assistants or work in teams in order to complete their tasks quickly.

A cook's job can be physically demanding, so keep that in mind as you select a career. Not only are

These peppers are on their way to being delicious, thanks to this sauté cook's talent.

cooks on their feet for most of the day, they are often working in hot kitchens, even during the summer. Cooks may at times have to lift large bags of ingredients (think about a 50-pound [23 kg] sack of potatoes) and must move around often to accommodate people coming in and out of the kitchen.

WHAT DOES IT TAKE TO BECOME A COOK?

Most cooking positions require that a candidate have a high school diploma before being hired. College isn't necessary, but hands-on experience is very important. It would be wise to apply only if you have some basic cooking techniques under your belt. Even if you are a whiz with chicken cordon bleu at home, it's unlikely that you will be able to walk into your first job and nab the head cook position.

Your best bet is to seek a part-time job as a line cook or short-order cook while still in school. By the time you finish high school, you will have a year or two of experience in a professional kitchen. This will help you immensely if you want to move up at your job or seek employment elsewhere.

PAY AND JOB SECURITY FOR COOKS

As with a restaurant manager, the area in which one lives, the kind of restaurant, and the number of patrons affect a cook's

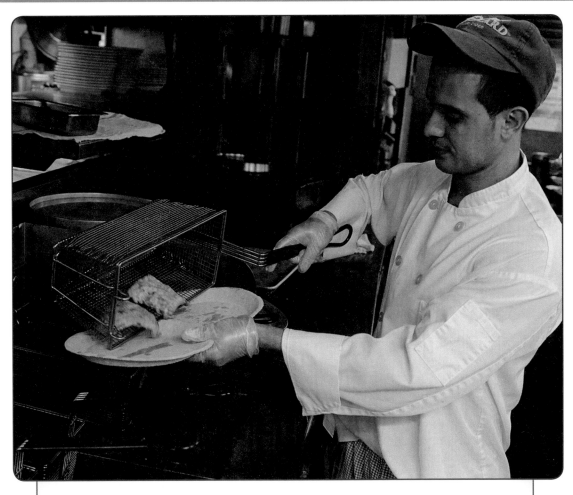

A line cook fries up some golden goodies for the customers of Boston's Union Oyster House, one of the oldest restaurants in the United States.

salary. Most cooks will tell you, too, that the amount of business a restaurant brings in influences salaries as well.

Experience is an important factor when it comes to making money as a cook. The lowest-level cooks will naturally be paid the least, but after a couple of years, a cook's seniority in the kitchen will lead to more responsibility and hopefully an increase in pay.

With the amount and diversity of restaurants out there, you should have no problem finding a job as a cook, as long as you're willing to learn the restaurant's recipes and follow its way of doing things.

Like other positions at restaurants, cook positions usually have a high degree of turnover, so that is one thing you'll have on your side as you seek employment. Keep in mind, though, that if business slows in an area, a cook may have to move to where the work is.

FOR MORE INFORMATION

ORGANIZATIONS

American Culinary Federation (ACF)
180 Center Place Way
St. Augustine, FL 32095
(904) 824-4468
Web site: http://www.acfchefs.org
This professional organization for chefs and cooks offers culinary competitions, certifications, a national apprenticeship program, regional and national events, publications, and more.

Canadian Restaurant and Foodservices Association (CRFA)
316 Bloor Street West
Toronto, ON M5S 1W5
Canada
(800) 387-5649
Web site: http://www.crfa.ca
The CRFA represents all sectors of the Canadian food service industry, including restaurants, bars, cafeterias, coffee shops, caterers, and more.

National Restaurant Association (NRA)
2055 L Street NW, Suite 700

Washington, DC 20036

(202) 331-5900

Web site: http://www.restaurant.org

The National Restaurant Association represents almost four hundred thousand restaurants, providing valuable resources and information to all levels of food industry employees.

BOOKS

Cohen, Wayne. *Cooking on the Line: From Food Lover to Professional Line Cook*. Chicago, IL: Larousse Churchill Publishing Corp., 2011.
This book provides a unique perspective on being a line cook from someone who serves up countless meals every day.

Crumpacker, Bunny. *How to Slice an Onion: Cooking Basics and Beyond: Hundreds of Tips, Techniques, Recipes, Food Facts, and Folklore*. New York, NY: Thomas Dunne Books/St. Martin's Press, 2009.
This is a great guide for beginning cooks.

Draz, John, and Christopher Koetke. *The Culinary Professional*. Tinley Park, IL: Goodheart-Wilcox Company, 2010.

The authors provide a comprehensive explanation of cooking techniques, equipment, and foods used in a professional kitchen.

Gold, Rozanne. *Eat Fresh Food: Awesome Recipes for Teen Chefs*. New York, NY: Bloomsbury Children's Books, 2009.
This cookbook offers healthy, tasty recipes that are easy for busy teens to prepare.

Locricchio, Matthew. *Teen Cuisine*. Tarrytown, NY: Marshall Cavendish, 2010.
This cookbook offers over fifty detailed recipes that are easy for cooking novices to tackle.

PERIODICALS

Cook's Country
America's Test Kitchen
17 Station Street
Brookline, MA 02445
Web site: http://www.cookscountry.com
This magazine is a great resource for delicious recipes and cooking tips.

Cook's Illustrated
America's Test Kitchen
17 Station Street
Brookline, MA 02445
Web site: http://www.cooksillustrated.com
Cook's Illustrated magazine is full of recipes, tips, equip-
    ment reviews, and other topics of interest for cooks.

WEB SITES

Due to the changing nature of Internet links, Rosen Publishing has developed an online list of Web sites related
to the subject of this book. This site is updated regularly.
Please use this link to access the list:

http://www.rosenlinks.com/CCWC/Cook

CHAPTER 4

SO YOU WANT TO WEAR A CHEF'S COAT?

These days, it seems as if any time you turn on the TV, you come across a reality show on which highly skilled chefs battle it out with their knives and whisks, competing to show who's the best in the industry. These popular shows have glamorized chefs and their artistic dishes, inspiring even the most novice cooks among us to pick up a frying pan. However, it takes more than just a knack for soufflé to become a chef. The road can be tough, but getting there is quite a delicious experience.

A chef earns his or her living by cooking for other people. What separates chefs from cooks, though, is that chefs are highly skilled professionals who are familiar with all aspects of food preparation. Although you don't need a traditional college degree to become a chef, you can't just walk into any old restaurant and become one, either. It requires a good deal of training and experience.

Being a chef is more than just a way to pay the bills. Chefs are artists. Instead of pens and paper, they use food to tell a story. Chefs spend countless hours devising, concocting, and conjuring amazing dishes. The results are a product of well-organized, creative, and efficient minds.

A FOOD LOVER'S DREAM

It's obvious that chefs must love food in order to be good at their jobs. Highly developed senses of taste and smell are essential, too. Being able to create, alter, blend, and execute subtle flavors is the key to separating yourself from the pack of professional and casual foodies out there.

Every chef in the kitchen functions as part of a team, so being able to work well with others is crucial. There are several kinds of chefs, all of whom have the common goal of keeping a restaurant kitchen running smoothly. A kitchen couldn't function without every chef's contributions. As such, all chefs are expected to be responsible and respectful of the tasks at hand and of their coworkers.

The executive chef, also known as the head chef, is at the top of a kitchen's food chain. A person in this position must be a true leader, as he or she helms all of the kitchen's operations and supervises the entire line of chefs as well. Believe it or not, executive chefs do very little actual cooking. Their attention is focused on creating recipes, planning menus, adhering to a budget, taking care of inventory, and overseeing

Celebrated chef Jean-Georges Vongerichten shops for fruits and vegetables for one of his restaurants. Many chefs visit farmer's markets to find inspiration for their dishes.

several other administrative tasks. Executive chefs are the end of the line as far as responsibility goes. They are account-able for everything that goes into and out of the kitchen. Executive chefs are in the position to receive both blame and

Famous chef Thomas Keller tastes a sauce at his restaurant Per Se in New York City. A good sauce can complete a meal and tie all of the ingredients together.

praise, but the positive aspects of the job are immensely satisfying and rewarding.

Directly under the executive chef is the sous chef, the executive chef's right-hand man or woman. The sous chef may be responsible for the actual cooking of a meal while the head chef supervises other tasks going on in the kitchen. Some sous chefs perform in place of the executive chef if he or she is away, and some exist in an apprentice role, watching and learning on the way to becoming an executive chef.

Next in line is the saucier the French word for "sauce cook." Sauciers are in the highest position of all the station cooks, although they are still subordinate to the sous chef and head chef. Their main job is to create sauces. In traditional kitchens, sauciers are almost like chemists, using five basic sauces in various combinations to concoct hundreds of different new sauces. Every saucier has his or her own special ingredients and measurements, which make the creations of every saucier unique. In addition to sauces, a saucier may prepare soups or stews and perhaps even sautés to order.

Switching gears (and ingredients) a bit, on the other side of the kitchen you'll find someone just as specialized as a saucier—the pastry chef. This chef's area of expertise lies in making desserts, everyone's favorite course! Pastry chefs usually have chef's training but have chosen to focus on the desserts, breads, and other baked goods that we all love. Pastry chefs may have the responsibility of creating a restaurant's dessert menu and conceptualizing and testing new recipes. Most pastry chefs gain experience in cooking meals before they choose to focus on desserts.

Garde-manger chefs are in charge of all cold food that comes off the line. Often considered one of the most demanding positions in the kitchen, the garde-manger preps dishes such as salads, hors d'oeuvres, and various parts of buffets. An artistic flare is helpful for this job, as garde-mangers may oversee plating of the food and may produce ice carvings for special occasions.

Prep cooks are not involved in the actual cooking of food. Instead, they prepare the ingredients of the meals on a planned menu. Tasks can range from peeling potatoes or

Pastry chefs work hard to make their desserts look as good as they taste.

shrimp to mincing garlic and chopping fresh herbs. Most prep cooks hope to become chefs, and this position is a great stepping-stone because it allows them to develop important skills and techniques, such as knife skills.

No matter what kind of chef you are, shifts are often long and arduous. It isn't an easy job. Most chefs work days that are twelve hours or longer, and they must be available for early mornings, late evenings, weekends, and holidays.

WHAT DOES IT TAKE TO BECOME A CHEF?

Although this career doesn't require a college degree, if you're thinking of becoming a chef, some sort of higher education or formal training is necessary. The quickest way to get on track as a chef is to go to culinary school. There are many schools in the United States and Canada that offer culinary programs. Culinary schools educate future chefs in the art and science of food preparation. Students spend most of their class time in an actual kitchen, gaining hands-on experience with classical dishes and kitchen equipment. Holding a degree from a culinary school shows potential employers that you already know the basics of food preparation and are prepared to jump right into the work of a kitchen.

Education isn't the only thing necessary to become a chef. It's widely understood that there is no true substitute for experience. As such, many chefs learn the old-fashioned way. They work their way through the ranks by watching and learning from the more experienced chefs in restaurant kitchens. This is especially true of entry-level chefs who wish to become executive chefs someday. Everyone starts somewhere before rising to the top!

If you have an aptitude for cooking and are not planning to attend a cooking school, try your hand working as a cook or a member of a line in a restaurant. Another option is to take occasional classes while you work in a restaurant to improve your skills.

PAY AND JOB PROSPECTS FOR CHEFS

Being a chef can be a lucrative career. As with all industries, entry-level positions always pay less than the top of the hierarchy. Working your way up through several different positions should be accompanied by a steady increase in salary. Additionally, the more specialized your skills are, the more you can attempt to negotiate after a job offer. For example, a chef with a culinary degree, pastry experience, and the demonstrable ability to make sauces will be able to demand more than a new chef who has just taken a few classes.

Ultimately, salaries for chefs vary. Factors in one's salary include restaurant size and location. A chef who cooks for one hundred customers in a busy city has the opportunity to make a larger income than one who works in a less populated area.

The amount and availability of jobs for chefs is good, and the U.S. Department of Labor predicts that it will remain this way for the next ten years. It's noted, however, that job competition will remain high in upscale restaurants and hotels, simply because the pay in these places is much higher than in the average restaurant.

Besides working in a traditional restaurant, chefs have the additional options of heading up cooking lines in hospitals, colleges, hotels, and casinos. Some chefs also decide to take their skills to the classroom and pass them on to a whole new generation of culinary whiz kids.

Like other food industry positions, there is a substantial amount of turnover among chefs, so the payoff can be great for dedicated and persistent people who stay involved long enough to nab the higher positions. Plus, continual learning helps chefs build their cooking repertoire and keep their skills fresh and up to date.

FOR MORE INFORMATION

ORGANIZATIONS

American Culinary Federation (ACF)
180 Center Place Way
St. Augustine, FL 32095
(904) 824-4468
Web site: http://www.acfchefs.org
This professional organization for chefs and cooks offers
culinary competitions, certifications, a national apprenticeship program, regional and national events,
publications, and more.

Culinary Institute of America (CIA)
1946 Campus Drive
Hyde Park, NY 12538
(845) 452-9600
Web site: http://www.ciachef.edu
The CIA is one of the best-known schools solely dedicated to culinary arts in the United States. It offers
associate's and bachelor's degree programs, as well as
certificate programs.

Le Cordon Bleu, Inc.
One Bridge Plaza North Suite 275

Fort Lee, NJ 07024

(201) 490-1067

Web site: http://www.cordonbleuusa.com

Le Cordon Bleu is a premier school for culinary arts and hospitality, with a number of locations worldwide.

U.S. Chef Association (USCA)

P.O. Box 1922

Carbondale, CO 81623

(855) 707-USCA [8722]

Web site: http://www.uschefassoc.com

This association is targeted toward chefs in the United States. It offers chef education and training, access to chef competitions, and other membership benefits.

BOOKS

Bittman, Mark. *How to Cook Everything: 2,000 Simple Recipes for Great Food*. Rev. 10th anniversary ed. Hoboken, NJ: Wiley, 2008.

Mark Bittman's award-winning cookbook has helped countless cooks with its easy-to-follow and deliciously simple recipes. This edition has been updated to reflect the latest tastes and cooking trends.

Bourdain, Anthony. *Kitchen Confidential: Adventures in the Culinary Underbelly*. New York, NY: Harper Collins, 2000.
The extremely famous insider's look into a restaurant kitchen has sold millions of copies since its original publication in 2000.

Child, Juila, Louisette Bertholle, and Simone Beck. *Mastering the Art of French Cooking, Volume One*. New York, NY: Alfred A. Knopf, 1961.
Julia Child brought French cuisine to America, making complicated techniques accessible and doable for the average home cook.

Colicchio, Tom. *Think Like a Chef*. New York, NY: Clarkson Potter, 2007.
Industry powerhouse Tom Colicchio deconstructs a chef's thought process, teaching the everyday cook how to elevate his or her dishes and techniques.

The Culinary Institute of America. *The Professional Chef*. Hoboken, NJ: Wiley, 2011.

The Culinary Institute's textbook is a perennial classic for culinary students and professional chefs.

McGee, Harold. *On Food and Cooking: The Science and Lore of the Kitchen*. Rev. and updated ed. New York, NY: Scribner, 2004.
A kitchen staple, professional chefs and home cooks alike turn to this book for an understanding of what food is, where it comes from, and how it is used to create unique and beautiful dishes.

Rombauer, Irma S., et al. *The Joy of Cooking: 75th Anniversary Edition*. New York, NY: Scribner, 2006.
One of the best-known cookbooks ever published, this book began as a collection of recipes from friends and relatives. The seventy-fifth anniversary edition features recipes that have been updated for the modern palate.

PERIODICALS

Bon Appetit
Condé Nast Publications
4 Times Square, Floor 5
New York, NY 10036
Web site: http://www.bonappetit.com

Bon Appetit is a monthly food and entertaining magazine that publishes recipes, cooking tips and techniques, and celebrity chef interviews.

Chef Magazine
233 N. Michigan Avenue, Suite 1780
Chicago, IL 60601
Web site: http://www.chefmagazine.com
This digital and print magazine is full of recipes, chefs' tips, interviews, and unique perspectives on life as a chef.

Food & Wine
1120 Avenue of the Americas
New York, NY 10036
Web site: http://www.foodandwine.com
This magazine publishes content on all aspects of the food industry, with a focus on recipes and expert tips.

BLOGS
Chef's Pencil
http://www.chefspencil.com
The *Chef's Pencil* blog is a source for recipes, articles, and information for all levels of chefs, cooks, and foodies.

Super Chef
http://www.superchefblog.com
This blog is devoted to following celebrity chefs and
their businesses.

WEB SITES

Due to the changing nature of Internet links, Rosen Publishing has developed an online list of Web sites related to the subject of this book. This site is updated regularly. Please use this link to access the list:

http://www.rosenlinks.com/CCWC/Cook

CHAPTER 5

WHAT DOES A CATERER DO?

So far, we've talked about careers that will keep you inside the four walls of a restaurant. There are also jobs that can take you out of the kitchen but still require a love of food. One career that offers this is catering.

Have you ever gone to a large event, like a wedding or a banquet? One of the best things about attending such an event is the food. But it took a lot of work for that food to get from the store to your stomach. The dedicated professionals behind this enormous task are caterers.

FEEDING AN ARMY—OR JUST A WEDDING

Catering is the business of providing food to a different location than where it's prepared. Caterers furnish food to people who can't or don't have time to make it themselves. Good caterers take principles from the professions of restaurant chefs, bakers, and food stylists and use them to host events for large groups that are both memorable and pleasing to the eye.

Catering isn't just about the food: it's about the experience, too. Here, expert cake creator Sylvia Weinstock matches a wedding cake to the event's atmosphere.

People often seek out catering services when they need food for a large group. "Large" is relative here. It can mean anything from five to five thousand people. As a caterer, you may prepare food for a small office lunch one day and a huge wedding or conference the next. The best thing you can do as a caterer is to accept business that is manageable for the size and scale of your operation.

There are many different levels of catering. Some people choose to cater in their spare time and run small businesses from their homes. There are also large companies (hotels, for instance) that may have whole catering teams. In recent years, fast-food and chain restaurants have begun to offer catering. Grocery stores do it, too. This is because demand for catering is high.

Caterers are hired for their expertise. Clients may have an idea of the food they would like at their event but value the creative menu and display suggestions of a caterer. People skills are also an important part of being a successful caterer. Imagine a situation in which a client requests several changes to a menu in a short period of time. This requires patience and understanding on the part of the caterer. Ultimately, if a client and caterer cannot communicate well, it may hurt the overall success of an event.

Caterers also need to adapt quickly. For instance, if a caterer's usual supplier of vegetables is closed or out of certain ingredients, he or she cannot tell a client that the menu has to be changed. People hire caterers because they expect important functions to go smoothly and professionally. They're paying money so that they don't have to think about issues like this.

The food that caterers serve can vary. Some clients may request only sandwich fixings for hungry executives at a

Caterers often prepare large quantities of food and then transport it to business gatherings.

board meeting. Others may want to serve a five-course French meal. Many caterers have professional cooking backgrounds that help them immensely. However, it's not just about the food. Caterers usually remain on hand at an event, providing dinnerware, setting tables, and tearing it all down at the end of the night. Many also provide waitstaff and bartenders.

No matter the size of an event, organization is key. Less than half of a caterer's work time is actually devoted to cooking. The rest is spent transporting food and hiring personnel. Some caterers do not own the majority of the equipment they use, so finding and renting special dishes and tools can be time consuming. If they are serving alcohol at a function, they may need to visit city hall to obtain a special license.

Catering can open doors to other interesting lines of work. The insight gained through providing meals to people sometimes inspires professionals to become personal chefs. Some caterers move on to event planning, which can involve hiring caterers and entertainment, or they may jump to other fields such as floral supply or equipment rental.

WHAT DOES IT TAKE TO BECOME A CATERER?

Many culinary schools offer catering classes, but they are not necessary for launching a career. Many people begin at home, experimenting with various types of cuisine in order to have a wide base of meals from which their clients can choose. Home catering businesses have very low overhead (operating costs), and people can do it part-time to test out the market in their area. Another option is to work a few hours a week for a small caterer in the area.

If you do start your own catering enterprise, be as aggressive as possible. Hit the pavement and post advertising. Talk to other businesses that sell supplies for special events, such as flower shops and liquor stores, to see what it takes to obtain clients. Creating a Web site or social media page is another great way to get the word out about your services.

Another way to explore the business is to seek employment at a hotel or a banquet facility. These businesses are very experienced in hosting special affairs, and the experience an aspiring caterer can obtain is invaluable. Working at establishments like these does not require the initial investment needed to start your own business.

Training for a prospective catering career does not have to begin in such a focused manner. Any time spent working in a

Caterers usually prepare food off-site, in their own kitchen or in the catering company's facility. Some food can be prepared on-site at an event.

restaurant is extremely helpful, from waiting tables to working on the chef's line.

PAY AND JOB PROSPECTS FOR CATERERS

If you're looking to make money as a caterer, the most lucrative way to do it is to be self-employed. Working from your kitchen and using your own supplies to prepare food for small events means the overhead costs are low. As you gain experience and clients, you may find yourself in a position to expand your business.

However, as with other small businesses, the income gained from catering is entirely dependent on finding clients. If your marketing is ineffective and doesn't generate enough clients, the business won't make money.

If you decide to work for a catering company, the pay depends on what services you perform. The goal is to work your way up to being an integral member of a hotel or private catering team.

The food service industry has become one of the most steadily growing industries in recent years. There are many ways to break into the catering business. There are always jobs available with established businesses, or you can create your own opportunity by branching out alone. If you come up with an interesting variation on the general field of catering and make a name for yourself, the future in this line of work can be very bright.

FOR MORE INFORMATION

ORGANIZATIONS

International Caterers Association (ICA)
3601 East Joppa Road
Baltimore, MD 21234
(410) 931-8100
Web site: http://www.internationalcaterers.org
The ICA is a nonprofit organization dedicated to mentoring, educating, and promoting professional caterers and their businesses.

National Association for Catering and Events (NACE)
9891 Broken Land Parkway, Suite 301
Columbia, MD 21046
(410) 290-5410
Web site: http://www.nace.net
The NACE promotes and represents caterers and event personnel and acts as a trusted resource for questions, information, and job news.

BOOKS

Crawford, Isis. *A Catered Birthday Party*. New York, NY: Kensington Publishing Group, 2010.

This intriguing tale of a catering event gone wrong sets the backdrop for a murder mystery.

Shiring, Stephen B. *Professional Catering: The Modern Caterer's Complete Guide to Success*. Clifton Park, NY: Delmar, 2014.
This book equips readers with all of the knowledge and tools needed to start a competitive catering business.

Thomas, Chris, and Bill Hansen. *Off-Premise Catering Management*. 3rd ed. Hoboken, NJ: Wiley, 2013.
This book includes many forms and checklists to use throughout the planning and execution stages of an event, as well as time-management tips. It also provides staffing and marketing ideas.

Weinberg, Joyce. *The Everything Guide to Starting and Running a Catering Business: Insider Advice on Turning Your Talent into a Lucrative Career*. Avon, MA: Adams Media, 2007.
Experienced caterer Joyce Weinberg gives expert advice on how to start and run your own catering business.

Wyler, Susan. *Cooking for a Crowd: Menus, Recipes, and Strategies for Entertaining 10 to 50*. Revised ed. Emmaus, PA: Rodale Books, 2005.

This classic guide provides all the information you need on cooking for a large number of people.

WEB SITES

Due to the changing nature of Internet links, Rosen Publishing has developed an online list of Web sites related to the subject of this book. This site is updated regularly. Please use this link to access the list:

http://www.rosenlinks.com/CCWC/Cook

CHAPTER 6

PERSONAL CHEFS: OUT OF THE KITCHEN AND INTO THE HOME

Imagine that you're a busy professional who spends a lot of time at the office, a parent who has no time to cook, or someone who simply doesn't know how to make the food you enjoy. How do you put dinner on the table? That's where personal chefs come in. These culinary artists are hired by different clients to prepare meals in the clients' home kitchens.

Personal chefs tend to be classically trained chefs who have experience working in restaurants, hotels, or catering. They may hold full-time jobs elsewhere and provide personal chef services in their spare time or on an as-needed basis for dinner parties and events. This position is ideal for a person who loves to cook yet prefers to do so on a small scale, without the stress of a high-pressure kitchen or demands of running a restaurant or catering business.

THE PERSONAL TOUCH

What distinguishes personal chefs from the other careers we've discussed is that they are their own bosses. Technically

As a personal chef, you may find yourself preparing meals in clients' homes. Many personal chefs enjoy the change of pace from a busy restaurant kitchen.

small business owners, personal chefs choose their own hours, rates of pay, and clientele.

Becoming an executive chef in a restaurant takes years of work. Until then, many chefs spend a good deal of time assisting head chefs, who ultimately decide which dishes will be served. Starting your own business puts you in charge of everything, including every foodie's dream: the chance to develop your own unique creations.

Personal chefs prepare food based on their clients' needs and preferences. One family may want comfort foods like meatloaf or pork chops, while a health-conscious couple may request a week's worth of low-calorie meals. Another special request may be to develop meals around a person's dietary restrictions or allergies. For example, if a child is lactose intolerant, a personal chef needs to adjust his or her menu accordingly. An important quality for a personal chef is versatility: with a broad knowledge of flavors, food preparation techniques, and menu planning, personal chefs can increase their client base—and ability to make money—significantly.

Personal chefs do way more than cook. They must follow a food budget and shop for the best and freshest ingredients, all while keeping their clients' preferences in mind. This could mean shopping at once for several different families that all have different budgets, menus, and volumes of food to receive. Hence, organizational skills are extremely important.

The majority of personal chefs do not decide to "wing it" when they arrive at their clients' houses—they come prepared with preplanned menus. Personal chefs usually prepare meals at the beginning of the week and leave the meals in the refrigerator or freezer to be reheated later. In this capacity, knowledge of food storage and advance prep is key.

The chance to have close working relationships and possibly friendships with one's employers is a great bonus

This personal chef has prepped meals ahead of time for her clients. She has included specific directions for reheating each dish.

in this line of work. Most personal chefs get the chance to see their clients frequently and develop relationships with the people who eat and enjoy their food. This is personally rewarding and helpful for feedback and networking. Some personal chefs may even live in the house of the family whose food they prepare. In these cases, they are referred to as private chefs.

Title aside, becoming a personal or private chef is a great option for an independent, driven person who loves to cook and share food with people he or she cares about.

WHAT DOES IT TAKE TO BECOME A PERSONAL CHEF?

To be a personal chef, you must be experienced in the art of cooking and have a thorough knowledge of food preparation, food storage, and nutrition. All of the aforementioned skills are what will land you clients. Keeping your customers is a different story. That's where people skills come in. Restaurants have kitchen doors to separate the staff from the clientele, and the two rarely collide. That line doesn't exist for personal chefs. Being friendly and flexible is a must.

You can become a personal chef without formal training. Take personal chef Renee Messina, for example. Most of her early professional experience was gained through regular office jobs. In her spare time, though, she loved to prepare meals for her family and friends. One day she came across an online posting by a family looking for a personal chef and decided to take a chance. As she puts it, "I had nothing to lose by reaching out to this potential client. All I needed was to show them I could cook well and meet their expectations—whatever they were. I knew I could do this without a culinary degree." Today, Messina runs a personal chef business in addition to her regular job. It allows her to earn extra money while doing something her full-time job can't provide: cooking and sharing food with other people.

On the other hand, many personal chefs are classically trained. They come to the job having studied at professional cooking schools, which arms them with formal training and a foundation for starting a business. Many personal chefs start by working in restaurant or hotel kitchens before setting out to become entrepreneurs. Experience is key regardless of the path you take, since your clients will choose to work with you based on your ability to deliver a great product.

Once you decide you're ready to strike out on your own as a personal chef, it may be a good idea to join a personal chefs association to help you find work in your field and meet people who have done the job for some time. Associations like these offer certification programs. The field is very competitive, and having some credentials will assist you in interviews with potential clients.

Many people hire personal chefs so that they don't have to plan meals and shop for ingredients. Those tasks become the chef's responsibility.

PAY AND JOB PROSPECTS FOR PERSONAL CHEFS

There are two factors to consider when thinking about a personal chef's income: time invested and number of clients served. Many personal chefs are paid hourly, while others are paid a set rate based on the number and frequency of meals they provide.

Location will greatly influence a personal chef's income. For example, a personal chef in New York City likely makes more than a personal chef in Kansas, simply because of the difference in the cost of living.

Personal chefs are in control of their own destiny, and as such, have the opportunity to make as much money as they want, given that the demand for the services is there.

People are getting busier and busier. The number of families with two working parents is growing. People are putting in long hours. Some people simply view cooking as a chore after a long day. The growing demand for personal chefs reflects this. In fact, in 2010, *Entrepreneur* magazine named private chef services as one of the fastest-growing businesses in the country.

Being able to provide families with a hot meal after a long day is a skill that is both appreciated and sought after. Decades ago, many people would have balked at the thought of paying someone else to cook them dinner at home. But today's busy culture is different. Now is a great time to pursue a career as a personal chef, as long as you prepare yourself for the demands of this unique service.

FOR MORE INFORMATION

ORGANIZATIONS

American Personal & Private Chef Association
  (APPCA)
4572 Delaware Street
San Diego, CA 92116
(800) 644-8389
Web site: http://www.personalchef.com
The APPCA is the largest professional trade association for personal and private chefs in the United States.

Culinary Business Academy
4801 Lang Avenue NE, Suite 110
Albuquerque, NM 87109
(800) 747-2433
Web site: http://www.culinarybusiness.com
The Culinary Business Academy is an educational institution that provides specialized training to help individuals succeed in the food industry.

U.S. Personal Chef Association (USPCA)
7680 Universal Boulevard, Suite 550

Orlando, FL 32819

(800) 995-2138

Web site: http://www.uspca.com

The USPCA is an organization dedicated to developing the professional chef industry, setting standards and guidelines for professionals at all levels.

BOOKS

Bouloud, Daniel. *Letters to a Young Chef*. New York, NY: Basic Books, 2003.

Featuring notes from the kitchen, advice, and recipes, this book is a great read for anyone interested in a culinary career.

Postolowski, Ellen. *It's Just Personal: A Personal Chef's Essential Guide to Shopping, Cooking, and Eating Smarter*. Garden City, NY: Morgan Jams Publishing, 2009.

Personal chef Ellen Postolowski offers a health-minded perspective on preparing meals for clients.

Tishman, Alex. *The Best Book on How to Become a Private Chef*. San Francisco, CA: Hyperink, 2010.

This book answers the common questions one may have when considering becoming a personal chef.

Wallace, Candy. *The Professional Personal Chef: The Business of Doing Business as a Personal Chef*. Hoboken, NJ: Wiley, 2007.
Written by the APPCA's founder and executive director, this is the definitive book on starting and running a personal chef business.

PERIODICALS

Bon Appetit
Condé Nast Publications
4 Times Square, Floor 5
New York, NY 10036
Web site: http://www.bonappetit.com
Bon Appetit is a monthly food and entertaining magazine that publishes recipes, cooking tips and techniques, and celebrity chef interviews.

Fine Cooking
The Taunton Press
63 South Main Street
P.O. Box 5506

Newtown, CT 06470-5506
Web site: http://www.finecooking.com
Fine Cooking is a print and online magazine for culi-
    nary professionals and foodies. Its Web site features
    a recipe finder and interactive forum for its users.

Gourmet
Condé Nast Publications
4 Times Square, Floor 5
New York, NY 10036
Web site: http://www.gourmet.com
This print and online magazine combines travel and a
    love of food, examining great food across the globe.

BLOGS

Calibilini Personal Chef's Blog
http://caliblini.com/blog
This blog, written by a personal chef, includes mouth-
    watering pictures and sample menus.

Chef Bill
http://www.chefbill.com
On this blog, personal chef "Chef Bill" shares his
    thoughts on the daily tasks he encounters.

Your Personal Chef
http://blogs.lowellsun.com/yourpersonalchef
Jessica Roy includes tasty recipes and photos in her
  blog, which is sure to inspire even beginning home
  cooks to try their hand at her delicious food.

WEB SITES

Due to the changing nature of Internet links, Rosen Publishing has developed an online list of Web sites related
to the subject of this book. This site is updated regularly.
Please use this link to access the list:

http://www.rosenlinks.com/CCWC/Cook

CHAPTER 7

BAKING SWEETS, TREATS, AND BREAD

Ahh, bread. Is there a better smell in this world than that of baking bread? It's homey, comforting, and mouthwatering. If it does have a competitor, it might be freshly baked cookies or a pan of muffins warming in the oven. You probably enjoy these things already. Now imagine being paid to work with them every day. That's what you can expect if you decide to become a baker.

Bakers produce some of the world's sweetest and most appealing treats. If you can see yourself transforming flour, eggs, sugar, and butter into everyone's favorite food items, then this may be the career for you. Read on to see how you can get into this kind of work.

A PIECE OF CAKE—OR IS IT?

Bakers are professionals who spend their days making delicious baked goods for customers to enjoy. Working in a bakery or bakeshop, bakers do much more than open a box

of cake mix and go to work. The key phrase for most bakers is "from scratch." This means that good bakers know the exact combination of ingredients that are needed to produce a birthday cake or several loaves of bread. They don't rely on convenience foods or prepackaged products to do a good job—and the taste proves it!

Bakers need a good eye for detail because they spend much of their time following recipes and weighing, measuring, and mixing ingredients. Believe it or not, much of baking comes down to chemistry. Bakers don't need a degree in science, though. They just need a basic understanding of how and why baking ingredients work together. Bakers differentiate themselves by improvising ingredients (within reason) or adding a special slant to a common recipe. The personal touches a baker adds to his or her products is what keeps people coming back to that specific bakery.

Bakers spend a lot of time around huge ovens that are extremely hot, so safety is a big concern in this profession. Every time bakers open an oven to put in or take out products, they risk burns or a flash of heat in the face. Bakers need to be mindful of their backs and legs, too. Large bags of flour, sugar, and cornmeal are heavy. Combined with the stress of standing on one's feet for ten to twelve hours a day, bakers run the risk of straining their backs from lifting and stooping often.

Mark Isreal, owner of Doughnut Plant in New York City, cuts out some of his bakery's famous donuts.

This is not a career for late sleepers. Many bakeries that open to the public at 6 AM have had their ovens working for a few hours before that. The early bird catches the worm, and in the case of bakers, they need to be up hours before everyone else in order to get ready for the morning rush. In addition to the early hours, the average baker at a local bakery works at least forty hours a week.

There are several kinds of work environments for bakers. Some bakers work in independent bakeshops serving local communities on a small scale. There is more creative freedom in this environment, since you'll likely be the only baker, or one of two or three. There are also job opportunities at chain stores that have a presence around the whole country. These bakers have to follow a predetermined recipe book. Deviating from these recipes can cost you

A master baker checks loaves of sourdough bread at Boudin Bakery in San Francisco.

your job, since the company bases its recipes on what the public wants and the brand image it wants to convey. Finally, bakers also have the option of working for large-scale bakeries in grocery stores or factories. The bakers in these places turn out large volumes of baked products.

Where you work determines the day-to-day job responsibilities. If you work for a large-scale operation, you'll be one of many with less responsibility; if you work for a local bakery, everything may rest on your shoulders. It all depends on where you'd feel most comfortable.

WHAT DOES IT TAKE TO BECOME A BAKER?

A college degree isn't necessary to become a baker, but experience is. Apprenticing is the best way to start a career in baking. An apprentice is a person who works under the supervision of a professional while he or she learns the basics of a job. At the beginning of your apprenticeship, you may be asked to fetch ingredients or perform only the most basic tasks. But as time goes on, you may be allowed to try your hand at some of the easier techniques. In the case of professional baking, watching and learning from an experienced baker will allow you to see how to accurately execute a variety of baked goods.

Apprenticeships are highly competitive and sought after because you get paid while learning from the best. However, they're not readily available, so it's a good idea to get a head start on the competition by searching for one as early as possible. Chances are you won't be decorating cakes when you start: most bakery helpers spend their hours on the job cleaning pots, rolling pins, and mixing bowls. You might also begin by working a part-time job at your local bakery or grocery

Alabama students make challah bread in their high school's culinary lab. Baking is a science as well as an art, so knowledge of the craft is key.

store. These places are always willing to take on students and young adults, especially if it can spark a lifelong interest in baking.

There are two other great places to seek experience. If you attend a vocational high school, you may be able to take a baking course. This kind of class will teach you the basics and expose you to specialized baking equipment. Take advantage of this option if it's available to you. It can give you insight into the profession and possible connections if you choose a career in baking.

As for the last option, it's simple. Bake at home! Invest a few dollars in cookbooks, watch baking shows, or look for recipes online. It's better to try and fail first in your own kitchen rather than make your first attempts in an actual bakery. Plus, bakeries are more likely to hire you if you can demonstrate some concrete skills. A delicious plate of cookies couldn't hurt, either!

PAY AND JOB PROSPECTS FOR BAKERS

The highest-paid retail bakers belong to unions. Unfortunately, not every business that employs bakers is unionized. You'll usually find unionized bakers in grocery stores and factories. Independent bakeshops and small-scale operations aren't likely to have unionized workers.

Most bakers are paid hourly, and the pay matches their experience. Expect to make minimum wage as an apprentice. Moving up from there, bakers will see pay increases based on how long they've been with the company. Note that some bakers choose to specialize in a craft such as cake decorating. These are the highest-paid bakers of all, since they have a highly sought-after skill. Cake decorators who create individual and artistic designs for each item can be very well paid. Bakers in this category are referred to as artisans. Pastry chefs also fall into this category.

Data from the U.S. Department of Labor says that there will be little to no change in the job outlook for bakers. It seems to be a steady industry. If anything, the rise in small bakeshops and pop-up cake and cupcake stores should increase the number of opportunities.

FOR MORE INFORMATION

ORGANIZATIONS

American Bakers Association (ABA)
1300 I Street NW, Suite 700W
Washington, DC 20005
(202) 789-0300
Web site: http://www.americanbakers.org
The American Bakers Association is the voice of the wholesale baking industry. It advocates for more than seven hundred companies around the country.

American Society of Baking (ASB)
P.O. Box 336
Swedesboro, NJ 08085
(800) 713-0462
Web site: http://www.asbe.org
The ASB facilitates interactions among professional, commercial bakers to help promote and foster career and industry development.

Independent Bakers Association (IBA)
P.O. Box 3731
Georgetown Station
Washington, DC 20027

(202) 333-8190
Web site: http://www.independentbaker.net
The IBA is a national trade association of independently
 owned bakeries.

Retail Bakers of America (RBA)
15941 Harlem Avenue, #347
Tinley Park, IL 60477
(800) 638-0924
Web site: http://www.retailbakersofamerica.org
This is a community of retail bakers, designed to be the
 go-to place for education, resources, and networking
 among bakers and bakery owners.

BOOKS

Betty Crocker Editors. *Betty Crocker Big Book of Cupcakes*.
 Hoboken, NJ: Wiley, 2011.
This fun and eye-catching cookbook features 175 differ-
 ent cupcake recipes, along with decorating tips.

Chattman, Lauren. *The Baking Answer Book: Solutions to
Every Problem You'll Ever Face; Answers to Every Question You'll Ever Ask*. North Adams, MA: Storey Publishing, 2009.

This book covers the gamut of baking questions and will help even the most novice baker navigate common problems.

Figoni, Paula I. *How Baking Works: Exploring the Fundamentals of Baking Science*. Hoboken, NJ: Wiley, 2011.
This book explores the chemistry behind baking.

Hamelman, Jeffrey. *Bread: A Baker's Book of Techniques and Recipes*. Hoboken, NJ: Wiley, 2013.
The updated version of this classic simplifies complex baking topics and techniques.

White, Karey. *For What It's Worth*. Springville, UT: Bonneville Books, 2012.
This charming, fictional book follows an aspiring cake shop owner.

PERIODICALS

Bake
Sosland Publishing Company
4800 Main Street
Kansas City, MO 64112
(816) 756-1000
Web site: http://www.bakemag.com

Bake magazine is free to any baking professional interested in keeping up with industry news and notes.

Bakers Journal
105 Donly Drive South
Simcoe, ON N3Y 4N5
Canada
(888) 599-2228
Web site: http://www.bakersjournal.com
This Canadian magazine focuses on the people and business developments in Canada's baking industry.

Dessert Professional
222 West 37th Street, 6th Floor
New York, NY 10018
Web site: http://www.dessertprofessional.com
This online and print magazine covers the intricacies of making delicious and eye-catching desserts.

BLOGS

Brown Eyed Baker
http://www.browneyedbaker.com
A self-taught baker shares a variety of delectable treats that she has made in her kitchen.

Teen Baker
http://teenbaker.blogspot.com
Written by a seventeen-year-old baking aficionado,
   you'll find recipes and photographs of blogger Lucy's
   baking adventures.

WEB SITES

Due to the changing nature of Internet links, Rosen Publishing has developed an online list of Web sites related to the subject of this book. This site is updated regularly. Please use this link to access the list:

http://www.rosenlinks.com/CCWC/Cook

CHAPTER 8

FOOD CO-OPS: A GROCERY STORE ALTERNATIVE

Think about your neighborhood. You probably have large grocery stores that offer all of their products year-round. These stores may be where you and your family do the majority of your grocery shopping. However, your town may also have smaller grocers and even something called a food cooperative.

Food cooperatives (also known as co-ops) are collectively owned grocery stores. Food co-ops are run and paid for by members, who sometimes have the opportunity to own a small piece of the business. Most co-ops consider themselves "buying agents," which means they exist as an alternate source of products for consumers. All co-ops are different, but they share the common values of teamwork and social and ethical responsibility regarding the food we eat. If you like to carefully consider what you eat and want to get involved with your local community, you should explore what your local food co-op has to offer.

Because members own and run food co-ops, they offer more locally sourced, ethically produced, and organic products than typical grocery stores.

A NONPROFIT PAYCHECK

The jobs at a food co-op are similar to the jobs found at a supermarket or large food store. For example, most co-ops have department managers and buyers. In some cases, a manager also does the buying for his or her department, whether it is produce, beauty aids, or baked goods. A good buyer/manager needs to know what is and isn't in stock. He or she also needs to know when the out-of-stock items will be available again. Department managers report to a general manager. This individual is responsible for the day-to-day running of the co-op, which can include processing payroll and dealing with employee concerns.

The best way to get your foot in the door at a food co-op is to volunteer. Most co-ops require that their members volunteer in order to enjoy the benefits of membership. By working as a co-op volunteer, you have the opportunity to become familiar with the routine. This exposure will make obtaining a paid position easier, since the staff will know you already and see that you are dedicated to their cause.

Vicki Reich is the food buyer at the Moscow Food Co-op located in Moscow, Idaho. But she didn't start off there. She actually began as a volunteer and worked her way up to her current position. Her path took two years and involved working as a maintenance person, delicatessen worker, baker, cashier, and nonfood buyer. "My job grew as the store grew," Reich says. "I used to work alone, but as the co-op expanded, I needed the help of the two assistants I have now."

Most co-op employees spend their share of time working in lower-level positions before graduating to better-paying

THE HISTORY OF CO-OPS

The idea of the food cooperative came about in the nineteenth century, across the Atlantic Ocean in the little town of Rochdale, England. A small group of individuals ran a cooperative as a way to alleviate the burden of everyone having to provide everything they needed on their own. The "Rochdale Pioneers," as they were called, emphasized sharing and community over complete self-sufficiency.

The idea eventually found its way to America. The number of food cooperatives exploded between the years of 1969 and 1979, with the total reaching close to ten thousand. Food cooperatives provided an organic, anticorporate alternative to traditional chain stores. In other words, cooperatives jibed with the "hippie" mind-set of many people in 1970s America.

The number of food co-ops began to wane as the years went on, but in the last decade they have slowly started to emerge again. If anything, co-ops have had a great influence on many modern food stores. Today, there are a number of popular all-organic grocery stores, and even big-box chains make an effort to carry organic and locally sourced food.

jobs. Take it from Reich, who had this to say: "The general manager of our co-op started as a volunteer. She worked her way up by performing well and having the desire to move up through the ranks."

People like working at co-ops because of the sense of community found there. Everybody is working for a common cause, and this creates a friendly and enjoyable atmosphere. Since co-ops are not run solely for profit, employees and customers have a say in their operations. Co-ops are run democratically. As an employee, you may be able to vote on hiring decisions, employee rules, and other management decisions. This is rarely found in other kinds of positions!

A drawback to working in a food co-op is that the focus is not on making money. As such, wages may be slightly less than in some other food-related jobs. However, the democratic principles on which a co-op is based, coupled with the fair and friendly environment, are a welcome change for

This manager works in a co-op with a very inviting, homey atmosphere.

many people. As Reich says, "If you can handle not being a millionaire and enjoy what you do, then I call that success."

WHAT DOES IT TAKE TO WORK AT A FOOD CO-OP?

The best way to get started at a food co-op is to simply go in and talk to the people who work there. They will be more than willing to give you an overview of the co-op and answer any questions you may have.

Before committing to a job or volunteer hours, it may be a good idea to sign up as a member and see if you enjoy the environment. If the membership fee is too much for you, ask if you can work for free for the experience. Training, as with many jobs in food markets, is accomplished through hands-on work.

PAY AND JOB PROSPECTS FOR CO-OP EMPLOYEES

Pay rates for employees of a co-op vary by position, location, and membership. Also, a larger, more established food co-op is more likely to pay a higher wage than a brand-new one. The manager of a co-op will earn a higher salary than buyers or cashiers. As stated before, food co-ops are likely to pay less

Working the cash register as an employee or volunteer allows you to interact with customers. It also helps you learn about the different products the co-op sells.

than other food stores, simply because the focus of the business is not profit or making money.

People are concerned about food integrity now more than ever. They need places that provide local, sustainable, and safe food, and co-ops answer this call. Co-ops need employees and volunteers to help further their mission, so finding a job in one shouldn't be difficult.

FOR MORE INFORMATION

ORGANIZATIONS

International Co-operative Alliance (ICA)
150 Route de Ferney
P.O. Box 2100
1211 Geneva 2
Switzerland
+41 22 929 88 38
Web site: http://2012.coop
The International Co-operative Alliance serves co-ops around the globe with information, resources, and the general promotion of the trade itself.

National Cooperative Business Association (NCBA)
1401 New York Avenue NW, Suite 1100
Washington, DC 20005
(202) 638-6222
This association works to protect, advance, and defend cooperative businesses and to ensure that consumers have access to cooperatives in the marketplace.

National Cooperative Grocers Association (NCGA)
14 South Linn Street
Iowa City, IA 52240
(866) 709-COOP [2667]
Web site: https://www.ncga.coop

This organization works to promote food co-ops around the country, aiming to bring them to the forefront of the natural foods industry.

Neighboring Food Co-op Association (NFCA)
P.O. Box 93
Shelburne Falls, MA 01370
Web site: http://nfca.coop
This association is a network of more than thirty co-ops in the New England area, working together to create a healthy, just, and sustainable food system.

BOOKS

Ackerman-Leist, Philip. *Rebuilding the Foodshed: How to Create Local, Sustainable, and Secure Food Systems.* White River Junction, VT: Chelsea Green Publishing, 2013.
The author showcases some of the most promising models for growing, processing, distributing, and selling sustainably grown food.

Cumbie, Patricia, and Margaret J. Goldstein. *How to Start a Food Co-op: A Guide from the Cooperative Grocers' Education Network.* Arcata, CA: Cooperative Grocers' Education Network, 2010.
This book provides an overview of the basic steps and procedures involved in starting a retail food co-op.

Davis, Alex, Diana Ellis, and Andy Remeis. *Dinner at Your Door: Tips and Recipes for Starting a Neighborhood Cooking Co-op*. Layton, UT: Gibbs Smith, 2008.
This book uses the "cooperative" mentality to show how sharing and pitching in with those around you can lead to tasty and convenient results at mealtime.

Watson, Linda. *Wildly Affordable Organic: Eat Fabulous Food, Get Healthy, and Save the Planet—All on $5 a Day or Less*. Cambridge, MA: Da Capo Press, 2011.
Learn how the foods we eat affect our world and the steps you can take to reduce your carbon footprint with your diet.

PERIODICALS

Cooperative Grocer
2600 East Franklin Avenue
Minneapolis, MN 55406
(612) 436-9182
Web site: http://www.cooperativegrocer.coop
Cooperative Grocer is a bimonthly trade magazine for food cooperatives in North America.

YES!
Positive Futures Network

284 Madrona Way NE, Suite 116
Bainbridge Island, WA 98110-2870
(800) 937-4451
Web site: http://www.yesmagazine.org
YES! is a nonprofit magazine that reports on social and
    environmental best practices. Its food section pro-
    vides informative articles and tips on food coopera-
    tives and the locally sourced food movement.

BLOGS

Park Slope Food Co-op Environmental Committee Blog
http://ecokvetch.blogspot.com
The Park Slope Food Co-op is a popular co-op based
    in Brooklyn, New York. Its environmental committee
    blog provides environmental news and tips on how
    to protect the planet.

WEB SITES

Due to the changing nature of Internet links, Rosen Publishing has developed an online list of Web sites related
to the subject of this book. This site is updated regularly.
Please use this link to access the list:

http://www.rosenlinks.com/CCWC/Cook

CHAPTER 9

PENS AND FORKS: THE ART OF FOOD JOURNALISM

Imagine a job in which you get paid to visit restaurants, eat their food, and then write about the experience. It sounds almost too good to be true, right? This is what food critics do for a living. They're paid to write fair, unbiased views of restaurants, which can either prompt diners to visit restaurants or maybe even scare them away. If you've ever read a restaurant review and thought you could write a better one, food critic may be the job for you.

There are countless perks to being a food critic. In fact, it might be one of the coolest gigs out there. Food critics usually have their meals paid for by their employers, and each new restaurant is a brand-new dining experience. You get to try a variety of dishes on the menu, including everything from appetizers to desserts. The real question is: who wouldn't want to make money by eating out and giving an opinion about it? Food critics have great jobs because they get to share their love of food and the enjoyment of eating it with others.

PLATE TO PAGE

Food critics must come to their job with two important qualities: a refined palate and strong writing ability. In this profession, writing may be the more important skill. People don't want to read reviews that describe a meal as just "good" or "OK"; food critics are expected to provide an insightful and well-thought-out account of their overall dining experience. A large vocabulary is also worth its weight in gold. Writing a sentence such as, "The chicken arrived

Deciding what to order is one of the best parts of a food critic's job.

shriveled and tough, its meat unyielding to my fork and knife," is much more interesting than simply saying, "The chicken was dry."

In addition to writing about the food itself, food critics report on the restaurant's service, ambiance, and décor, since dining out involves more than just a meal. What separates a good food critic from a great food critic is the ability to make readers feel as if they were experiencing everything firsthand. Critics do this by reporting on small details: they might describe how the food was plated or mention something noteworthy about the service they received. If the food is great, but the waiter accidentally spills a drink all over a reviewer's new shirt, the review may not favorable.

As an aspiring food critic, you'll want to arm yourself with a solid understanding of food and the way it's prepared. Culinary school is not required, but a few short courses here and there may help. Many food critics were once chefs or cooks themselves. Knowing how food is prepared gives food critics a better idea of how a meal should taste, including the ability to identify good and bad aspects of certain dishes. Plus, having some experience with food makes you an authority in the eyes of readers. They're more likely to trust your opinion if you have more knowledge on the subject than they do.

Ruth Reichl, a well-known *New York Times* food critic, wrote a successful memoir about her career. She often ate meals in disguise so that restaurants wouldn't spot her and treat her differently.

THE SECRET LIFE OF A CRITIC IN DISGUISE

Garlic and Sapphires

Ruth Reichl

This profession is not for the faint of heart (or stomach). Good critics must be able to eat adventurously and often. They may eat a standard steak-and-potatoes meal at one restaurant and then fish eggs at another. A food critic may need to make multiple trips to the same eatery if its menu is varied. If you're a picky eater, this definitely isn't the right field for you.

Food critics always have to keep one thing on their minds: their weight! A job that involves eating, eating, and more eating directly affects the waistline. Food critics have to be careful to not let their job compromise their health. If you choose to go into this profession, you may want to invest in both a computer *and* running sneakers!

Now that you know the skinny on being a food critic, where can you find work? Local news shows, radio programs, newspapers, and magazines are the most common employers. The average critic with a secure position reviews one or two restaurants per week. This may or may not be a livable salary. Therefore, many critics review food for several different publications or have another job in addition to critiquing restaurants.

One final word: it's important to be honest and fair. The word "critic" doesn't mean that the writing always has to be negative. If the food is not very good, a wise critic might provide constructive criticism or give suggestions on how to improve a certain meal or restaurant.

WHAT DOES IT TAKE TO BECOME A FOOD CRITIC?

There is no such thing as a degree in food criticism. This is great news for the person who doesn't want to go to college. However, writing skills are a must, so some education is probably necessary.

To enter this line of work, continually work on your writing and knowledge of food. Joining your school's newspaper

Reviewing restaurants is a tasty job, and it's a social one, too. Many critics, including these food bloggers, dine with a partner, which helps them sample as many dishes as possible.

or writing club is a great way to start building a portfolio. These clubs may let you write local restaurant reviews for them. For something a little less formal, you can check out the various restaurant and business review Web sites, such as Yelp! and UrbanSpoon. These Web sites give regular people the opportunity to put in their two cents about a restaurant. This could be a great way to try your hand at reviewing restaurants, since other users will often tell you if they find your comments helpful.

Another avenue is to volunteer part-time at a local newspaper or television show that reviews food regularly. Food critics usually write for the "Weekend" or "Lifestyles" sections of newspapers. Try a few sample reviews on your own, and see what the local newspaper or magazine editor thinks. This is a good way to get solid and honest feedback on your writing.

If none of these avenues are open to you, browse through cookbooks and books on food. Subscribe to a food magazine and read its reviews, or watch food shows on TV. The key is to get involved in this industry early. You may want to try cooking exotic foods at home or experimenting with gutsy choices at nearby restaurants. Try as many different types of food as possible to expand your palate.

Remember, if people like their jobs, they usually like to talk about them. Go to a television station or newspaper.

Contact a food critic via e-mail and ask him or her questions about his or her job. The critic may know about employment opportunities or may be able to advise you on how to get started.

PAY AND JOB PROSPECTS FOR FOOD CRITICS

Food critics' salaries differ, depending on the publisher of their reviews. A critic whose work is placed in a monthly national magazine may be able to make more money than someone who writes for the county newspaper. Food critics are writers, and they can be paid per word or per article. This is determined by an individual publication. Contact various magazines or papers to see what each one offers food writers.

Competition is very tough in this profession—who wouldn't want to eat great food and get paid to write about it? More food critics can be found in areas with larger populations because there are more publications that employ them. A small city may have only one newspaper, but large cities like Los Angeles, Toronto, or Chicago may have three or four daily publications. Regardless, the key is to decide early on that you want to be a food critic and devote your time to getting there.

FOR MORE INFORMATION

ORGANIZATIONS

Association of Food Journalists (AFJ)
7 Avenida Vista Grande
Suite B7, #467
Santa Fe, NM 87508
(505) 466-4742
Web site: http://www.afjonline.com
The AFJ is a networking and educational organization that promotes friendship and professional development among food journalists.

International Food, Wine & Travel Writers Association (IFWTWA)
1142 South Diamond Bar Boulevard, #177
Diamond Bar, CA 91765-2203
(877) 439-8929
Web site: http://ifwtwa.org
This organization is a global network of journalists who cover hospitality and lifestyle topics, including food.

Society of Professional Journalists (SPJ)
Eugene S. Pallium National Journalism Center
3909 North Meridian Street

Indianapolis, IN 46208

(317) 927-8000

Web site: http://www.spj.org

This professional society has resources on its Web site geared specifically toward journalism students and aspiring writers.

BOOKS

Hughes, Holly. *Best Food Writing 2012*. Boston, MA: Da Capo Press, 2012.
Editor Holly Hughes presents a collection of the most interesting food writing published in a year.

Jacob, Dianne. *Will Write for Food: The Complete Guide to Writing Cookbooks, Blogs, Reviews, Memoir, and More*. Revised and updated ed. Cambridge, MA: Da Capo Lifelong, 2010.
This book is a must-have how-to guide for food writing.

Reichl, Ruth. *Garlic and Sapphires: The Secret Life of a Critic in Disguise*. New York, NY: Penguin Books, 2005.
World-renowned food critic Ruth Reichl recounts her experience as a food critic and the art of writing fair restaurant reviews.

Senyei, Kelly. *Food Blogging for Dummies*. Hoboken, NJ: Wiley, 2012.
This step-by-step guide shows you how to launch and run your own food blog.

BLOGS

Average Joe: Food Critic
http://traveragejoe.blogspot.com
This blog is great example of how you can publish your food reviews online.

WEB SITES

Due to the changing nature of Internet links, Rosen Publishing has developed an online list of Web sites related to the subject of this book. This site is updated regularly. Please use this link to access the list:

http://www.rosenlinks.com/CCWC/Cook

CHAPTER 10

FOOD IS ART, TOO: FOOD STYLISTS AND PHOTOGRAPHERS

You may be the type of person who likes both food and art. Did you know there are careers that satisfy both interests? It's all about the art of food styling. Food styling can involve everything from making food to plating it to photographing it. Food is professionally photographed or filmed for magazines, books, advertisements, and movies. Food stylists and photographers are responsible for creating the images that make us hungry. If you want a job in which you can combine a love of art with a love of food, you may find yourself pursuing one of these careers.

STYLING YOUR WAY TO THE TOP

First and foremost, food stylists are cooks who handle all food items involved in a food photography shoot. They obtain ingredients, cook them, and ensure that the prepared food remains ready to be photographed, maintaining a uniform look throughout a busy day of shooting.

Food stylists turn food into photo-worthy art using a variety of tools, some of which don't even belong in the kitchen.

Preparing food for photographing requires many different skills. These skills fall somewhere between art and science. Food stylists need to truly understand the properties of the foods they cook. They must know things such as how far in advance an item can be made, or if something will lose its color over time. This is especially relevant when working with foods that will melt or spoil if not refrigerated.

The conditions on photo sets can be tough on food. Imagine what a pint of ice cream looks like after spending hours under the glare of hot lights! In cases like these, food stylists may have to chemically alter the food they've prepared. This is where science and art start to mix. A slight knowledge of chemistry can help out immensely; a few shakes of salt or a drop or two of a preserving liquid can help extend a food's life.

Food stylists are responsible for fun tasks such as plating food, or arranging all of a dish's components in an attractive way. The photographers then capture these arrangements and turn them into the mouthwatering images we see all around us. Think about all the images you see in a food magazine or restaurant menu. They make you hungry for a

A FOOD STYLIST'S TOOLBOX

Food stylists need to be ready for everything, since the entire shoot depends on them. Many stylists carry an ordinary fishing tackle box of supplies, but the contents are a far cry from what a fisherman needs. Most of the items in the tool kit don't have anything to do with food. Here are some items a food stylist typically keeps at hand:

- **Nonfood supplies.** These include paper towels, tweezers, toothpicks, cotton swabs, razor blades, oil, paintbrushes, electric mixer, blowtorch, spray bottle, hotplate, ice chest or cooler, cutting board, knives, sponges, ice cream scoop, measuring spoons and cups, glue, plastic ice cubes, paint stripper, pins, glycerin, and erasers.
- **Food supplies.** These include pepper, instant potatoes, jam, jelly, marmalade, flour, rice, maple syrup, parsley, salt, cinnamon, oregano, and kitchen bouquet (a sauce for browning and seasoning).

reason. Food stylists and photographers are paid to elevate the average dinner plate into a work of art.

Food stylists and photographers report to clients. A typical client can be a local restaurant, food blog, newspaper, or magazine. Some publications employ several food stylists and photographers to cover different categories of food, or different spreads they want to produce.

Whether you're employed by a large or small business, or even if you freelance, clients usually want the food to look

Styling and photographing food is similar to doing a modeling shoot—with food as the star.

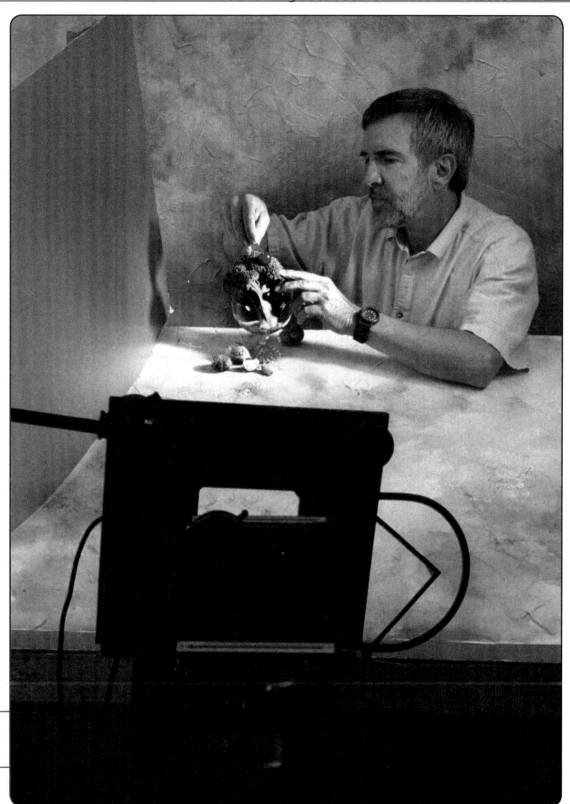

like it has just been prepared. This projects an appealing image to customers, which ultimately brings in business. These demands mean that no food stylist travels too far without a kit of ingredients and tools to handle any situation.

Stylists must be able to work as members of a team. They work with photographers, art directors, and the client who is paying for the photos or filmed food. Some stylists may have assistants to help clean the cooking items or carry equipment.

WHAT DOES IT TAKE TO BECOME A FOOD STYLIST OR PHOTOGRAPHER?

Experience in cooking and baking is very important for anyone who would like to try his or her hand in this field. The experience can come from different sources. Some food stylists have spent time as personal chefs or restaurant cooks; some have attended culinary schools. Most culinary or cooking schools offer courses in food styling but not full degrees. This is an advantage if you do not want to go to college.

Another important step toward working with food as art is apprenticing. Many hopeful stylists seek employment under the instruction of experienced veterans. After that, they can become an apprentice. Cooking skills are important for stylists (less so for photographers), but the most important aspect of these professions is presentation. One way to

Food photographers and stylists must have an eye for detail. The littlest finishing touches can make or break an image.

become proficient in either of these roles is to watch someone perform in his or her actual work environment.

Working for a seasoned stylist or photographer will give you practical experience and help you develop a portfolio, which you'll need to shop your work around when you strike out on your own. Learning all of the ins and outs of the profession can be time consuming, so be patient.

PAY AND JOB PROSPECTS FOR FOOD STYLISTS AND PHOTOGRAPHERS

As with other food-related careers, the income of a food photographer or stylist depends on his or her location. There is more work to be found in larger cities. (Are you starting to notice a trend?) One reason for this is that many magazine publishers and television and movie companies are based in more densely populated areas, like New York or Los Angeles.

Food stylists in cities are likely to make more money than professionals in other locales. Assistant salaries are far lower than those of full-fledged stylists or photographers, but this varies by employer.

Job prospects in food styling for print publication seem to be more plentiful and steadier than opportunities in television advertising and movies. More and more culinary schools are adding food styling to the courses they offer.

Photography is a little different in that it's possible to obtain a degree in photography. If you are interested in photography, you can put together a portfolio of your work. Even if it's not all focused on food, you can present this to a potential client as proof of your abilities.

FOR MORE INFORMATION

ORGANIZATIONS

American Society of Media Photographers (ASMP)
150 North 2nd Street
Philadelphia, PA 19106
(215) 451-2767
Web site: http://asmp.org
The ASMP has a group dedicated specifically to culinary
   and food photographers.

Culinary Institute of America (CIA)
1946 Campus Drive
Hyde Park, NY 12538
(845) 452-9600
Web site: http://www.ciachef.edu
The CIA is one of the best-known schools solely dedicated to culinary arts in the United States. It offers courses in and resources related to food styling.

Professional Photographers of America (PPA)
229 Peachtree Street, NE
Suite 2200
Atlanta, GA 30303
(404) 552-8600

Web site: http://www.ppa.com
Professional Photographers of America is an organization dedicated to advancing photographers in all sectors of the industry, including food photography.

BOOKS

Custer, Delores. *Food Styling: The Art of Preparing Food for the Camera*. Hoboken, NJ: Wiley, 2010.
Delores Custer, a food stylist with over thirty years of experience, shares her insider perspective on the industry.

Dujardin, Helene. *Plate to Pixel: Digital Food Photography & Styling*.Hoboken, NJ: Wiley, 2011.
This book gives you a peek into styling and photographing dishes in the digital age.

Vivaldo, Denise. *The Food Stylist's Handbook*. Layton, UT: Gibbs Smith, 2010.
Acclaimed food stylist Denise Vivaldo shares her trade secrets in her book.

Young, Nicole S. *Food Photography: From Snapshots to Great Shots*. Berkeley, CA: Peachpit Press, 2012.

This book covers everything you'll need to know about getting started as a food photographer.

PERIODICALS

Bon Appétit
Condé Nast Publications
4 Times Square, Floor 5
New York, NY 10036
Web site: http://www.bonappetit.com
Bon Appétit is famous not only for its content but also for its interesting food images.

Food & Wine
American Express Publishing
1120 Avenue of the Americas
New York, NY 10036
Web site: http://foodandwine.com
This print and online magazine contains recipes accompanied by attractive images.

Martha Stewart Living
601 West 26th Street
New York, NY 10001-1101
(212) 827-8000

Web site: http://www.marthastewart.com
This print and online magazine deals with many aspects of entertaining with food. It includes beautiful food photography and food styling tips.

BLOGS

Learn Food Photography and Food Styling
http://www.learnfoodphotography.com
This blog is a great resource for articles, tips, and tricks related to this interesting culinary profession.

Photography 101, "Working with Food Stylists."
http://psd101.blogspot.com/2011/08/working-with-food-stylists.html
This blog entry gives a thorough breakdown of how food photographers and stylists work together.

WEB SITES

Due to the changing nature of Internet links, Rosen Publishing has developed an online list of Web sites related to the subject of this book. This site is updated regularly. Please use this link to access the list:

http://www.rosenlinks.com/CCWC/Cook

GLOSSARY

AMBIANCE The character and atmosphere of a particular setting, such as a restaurant or hotel.

APPRENTICE A person who learns a trade from a skilled employer.

CELEBRITY CHEF A chef who has risen to the top of the food industry based on his or her talent and personality. Celebrity chefs are usually seen on TV and in magazines, and many write popular cookbooks.

CLIENTELE The customers of a business, such as a bar, shop, or restaurant.

COOPERATIVE A farm, business, or other organization that is owned and run jointly by its members, who share the profits or benefits.

COST OF LIVING A measure of how expensive it is to live in a certain area.

CRITIQUE To provide a detailed analysis or assessment of something.

CULINARY Of or for cooking.

CUSTOMER SERVICE The assistance and courtesy given to customers before, during, and after a purchase.

ENTRY-LEVEL Suitable for inexperienced workers who are just starting out in a career field.

FOOD BLOG An online informational site consisting of posts about food, recipes, restaurants, etc.

FOODIE A person who is highly interested in food, ingredients, proper preparation, and food trends.

GARDE-MANGER A chef who directly handles and prepares cold food.

LUCRATIVE Producing a great deal of profit.

NOVICE A person new to a field or profession.

PALATE A person's appreciation for taste and flavor.

PORTFOLIO A collection of work samples, photographs, documents, or other items that display a person's professional skills.

REPERTOIRE A stock of skills that a person has learned and is prepared to demonstrate.

SAUCIER A chef who prepares sauces.

SAUTÉ To cook quickly in a little bit of fat, such as butter or oil; a dish prepared in this manner.

SENIORITY The state of being older or in a higher position or status than someone else.

SOUFFLÉ A lightly baked caked made with egg yolks and beaten egg whites. Soufflés can be sweet or savory.

SOUS CHEF The chef who ranks directly under the executive or head chef and is second in command in the kitchen.

SUSTAINABILITY The quality of being able to use a resource without depleting all of it.

TURNOVER The rate at which employees leave a workforce and are replaced with new hires.

UPSCALE Relating to or appealing to affluent customers; luxurious.

VOCATIONAL Directed at a particular occupation or set of job skills.

INDEX

ABOUT THE AUTHOR

Sarah Machajewski is a self-proclaimed foodie and novice home cook whose experience in the food industry has taken her in and out of several restaurant kitchens. Now a writer by trade, her love of food and writing made researching this topic fun and hunger-inducing (and may have even inspired her to write a restaurant review or two).

PHOTO CREDITS

Cover, p. 3 ollyy/Shutterstock.com; p. 7 Ross Durant Photography/FoodPix/Getty Images; p. 10 mangostock/Shutterstock.com; pp. 12, 92–93 Justin Sullivan/Getty Images; pp. 16, 37, 82 Bloomberg/Getty Images; pp. 24–25 Helen H. Richardson/Denver Post/Getty Images; p. 26 Blend Images/Ronnie Kaufman/Larry Hirshowitz/the Agency Collection/Getty Images; p. 29 Blend Images/Shutterstock.com; pp. 40–41 Jetta Productions/Iconica/Getty Images; pp. 43, 51 Boston Globe/Getty Images; pp. 52–53 Maurice Rougemont/Gamma-Rapho/Gettty Images; pp. 55, 131 The Washington Post/Getty Images; p. 66 Jodi Cobb/National Geographic Image Collection/Getty Images; pp. 68–69, 77, 79, 90, 95, 104, 109, 119, 129 © AP Images; p. 71 Sacramento Bee/McClatchy-Tribune/Getty Images; p. 107 Don Treeger/The Republican/Landov; p. 115 © Rosenstrauch/Contra Costa Times/ZUMA Press; p. 117 Business Wire/Getty Images; pp. 126–127 © El Nuevo Dia/GDA/ZUMA Press; cover and interior design elements © iStockphoto.com/pialhovik (banner), © iStockphoto.com/David Shultz (dots), Melamory/Shutterstock.com (hexagon pattern), Lost & Taken (boxed text background texture), VoodooDot/Shutterstock.com (chapter opener pages icons.)

Designer: Brian Garvey; Editor: Andrea Sclarow Paskoff; Photo Researcher: Amy Feinberg